Mexican Food Made Easy

By Juanita Trejo-Beverly

Artwork by Juanita Trejo-Beverly

Dedication

This book is dedicated to my beautiful Mother

Angelina Arriaga Rojas

As a child, my Mother was my inspiration for Art, Sewing, Gardening and Cooking. She was always a loving teacher to me. I will always remember especially as a young girl growing up in our home and cooking along side her in her kitchen...she would teach me her special recipes with great loving guidance. I thank my creative Mother and I also must thank my talented Father for inspiring me to sing as well. As loving parents, they blessed me and my brothers and sisters with so many great gifts and talents. I will always love and cherish all of our wonderful creative memories spent together.

I will love you always and forever,

Juanita

Introduction

Around the age of 12, my mother started introducing me to sewing, crocheting, and embroidery. I always admired the way my mother could create and cook anything that she put her mind to. She was very talented and gifted. We would show her a photo of a dress design and she would be able to make it for us kids without needing any type of pattern. She was quite amazing.

She would make so many beautiful meals for our family of 8 with such great ease, and with whatever ingredients she had within her pantry. I remember one day asking her to please start teaching me how to cook some of my favorite dishes. She replied by asking me which dishes did I want to learn to cook first? I of course wanted to learn how to cook my most favorite dish, her delicious *Creamy Red Enchiladas!* I remember inviting some two young male Missionaries from our church to come over for lunch to be my taste testers (I never told them I was going to be the actual cook). I remember saying to my mother, that if the Enchiladas did not turn out good, would she mind terribly taking the "blame" for me...*please!?* But I also asked "if, the Enchiladas turn out great, please let our guests know that I had made the Enchiladas!". Well, my two guests arrived and they were seated at our table and we started serving them the Enchiladas… my mother and I sat down with them as I intently watched them take their first bite, they savored the flavors…..and then they announced that they loved the Enchiladas!!! Hurray, I felt so relieved that I had not ruined my mothers beautiful recipe! I was so proud of my first attempt to cooking! My mother was certainly very proud of me that day. Personally, I think she just made sure either way that nothing was overlooked (while she supervised my cooking) so that my first cooking presentation would be a memorable and positive one! Ever since that day, I continued learning more from her on how to cook many of her beautiful dishes. As I grew up and started working and living on my own, it became a little bit more challenging for me to cook for what seemed like "long hours" preparing all of those ingredients for my childhood favorite dishes. Years later, I began to implement creative new ideas in making her recipes a little more easier to prepare while still retaining those authentic flavors within each of her beautiful recipes. I also tried taking a more healthier approach by using olive oil and creating additional healthy and some refreshing recipes of my own. I hope you will enjoy these lovely "easy to make" recipes!

With love,
Juanita "Jane" Trejo-Beverly

First published in the USA 2012

Produced by Juanita Trejo-Beverly
Naples, Florida

© 2012 Juanita Trejo-Beverly

Book Cover: Robert Trejo Martinez &
Juanita Trejo-Beverly

Inside Book Design: Juanita Trejo-Beverly
Artwork: Juanita Trejo-Beverly
Recipes: Angelina Arriaga Rojas & Juanita Trejo-Beverly
Photographs: Juanita Trejo-Beverly

All rights reserved. No part of this publication may be reproduced,
stored in a retrieval system, or transmitted in any form
or by any means, electronic, mechanical, photocopying,
recording, or otherwise, without the prior permission
of the copyright owner.

Printed in the USA

Table of Contents

Appetizers:

Guacamole
Pico De Gallo
Pico De Gallo with Tuna
Pico De Gallo with Avocado
Mexican Style Shrimp Cocktail

Soups:

Spicy Jalapeno Lime Noodle Soup
Spicy Shrimp & Potato Soup
Spicy Pinto Bean Soup
Spicy Black Bean Soup
Spicy Corn Soup

Main Dishes:

Spicy Red Salsa Enchiladas
Creamy Red (non-spicy) Enchiladas
Chicken Tacos
Tostadas with Refried Beans (Chicken or Shrimp)
Fidello (Mexican Pasta)
Mole (Mexican Gravy with Chicken)
Chicharones Con Chili (Pork Rinds with Chili Peppers)
Nopalitos (Tender Cactus)

Mexican Food Made Easy

A tribute to wonderful memories
of love & laughter shared with
family and friends from
our table to yours.

~JTB

Appetizers

"Guacamole"

Ingredients:

2 Ripe Haas Avocados
1/2 Cup of finely chopped White Onion
1/2 Cup of chopped Plum Tomatoes
1 Fresh Serrano Pepper or, 1 Fresh Jalapeno Pepper Chopped (your preference)
This all depends on how spicy you desire the Guacamole
15 Strands of finely chopped fresh Cilantro
Freshly squeezed Lime Juice (Juice from 1 Lime but add more if needed)
Salt (as desired for good taste)

Preparation:

This is a great appetizer and a very healthy snack as well. If you need to make this dish an hour in advance, there is a cool "trick" you should learn in order to keep the Avocado and Guacamole looking "fresh". Once the Avocado has already been opened, keep the "Avocado pit" in the bowl with the Guacamole *(once it has already been prepared),* as this will keep the Guacamole looking green and fresh before serving it to your guests.

Otherwise, when you are ready to make fresh Guacamole: Slice each half into long slices so you can then cut the avocado into small cubes (from the already cut slices), place the Avocado slices into a bowl to mash together with a fork. Add chopped onions, chopped tomatoes, chopped Jalapenos or, Serrano peppers, add the Lime juice and then add salt for your desired taste. Serve fresh and enjoy with some corn tortillas chips! Enjoy!

Presentation of my
"Guacamole"

This recipe serves two people.
Adjust recipe according to how many people you will serve.

"Pico De Gallo"

Ingredients:

2 to 3 Large Plum Tomatoes chopped
1/2 Cup finely chopped White Onions
1 to 2 finely chopped fresh Jalapenos Peppers
15 strands of finely chopped Cilantro
Freshly squeezed Lime Juice (from 1 to 2 Limes)
Salt (as desired for good taste)
1/3 Cup of Chicken Broth, or Water (I prefer Chicken Broth for extra flavor)

Preparation:

Bring all of the Vegetable ingredients together into a medium size bowl to mash all of them together with a fork or, you can use a "potato masher" to make it easier for you if making large amounts.

Add the Chicken broth, the Lime juice into the mixing bowl with the chopped Tomatoes, Cilantro, Jalapenos, Onions and mash them all together. Add salt for good taste. Once all the vegetables are mashed together, taste again to be sure it has enough lime juice as well.

I discovered that the Chicken Broth adds extra flavor to this Salsa (much better than basic water). You can add more hot peppers and/or, more Lime juice according to your preference.
Serve this Pico De Gallo Salsa with some Tortillas Chips. Enjoy!

Presentation of my

"Pico De Gallo"

This recipe serves 1 to 2 people.
Adjust according to how many people you will serve.

Pico De Gallo with Tuna

Ingredients:

2 to 3 finely chopped Plum Tomatoes
1/2 of a finely chopped white Onion
15 strands of finely chopped Cilantro
1/2 teaspoon of Pepper
Salt (as desired for good taste)
Freshly squeezed Lime juice (1 to 2 Limes)
2 to 3 Tablespoons of "Tapatio" Hot Sauce
2 Small cans of Tuna (5 oz. cans)
1 to 2 Avocados

Preparations:

In a medium size bowl mix your tuna in with the lime juice, Tapatio hot sauce, salt and pepper and mix these together.

Now bring all of the vegetable ingredients together into the Tuna bowl to mix together with a fork to bring all these flavors together.

This dish is great as a healthy snack or, refreshing healthy salad. You can add more of the Tapatio hot sauce and more Lime juice too. Enjoy serving this salsa tuna salad with sliced Avocados, Blue Corn Tortillas chips or, Water Crackers. Enjoy!

Presentation of my
Pico De Gallo with Tuna

Serve with a wedge of Lime and some Tapatio hot sauce.

This dish serves 1 to 2 people.
Adjust according to how many people you wish to serve.

Pico De Gallo over Avocado

Ingredients:

2 to 3 finely chopped Plum Tomatoes
1/2 of a finely chopped white Onion
15 strands of finely chopped Cilantro
1/2 teaspoon of Pepper
Salt (as desired for good taste)
Freshly squeezed Lime juice (1 to 2 Limes)
2 to 3 Tablespoons of "Tapatio" Hot Sauce
2 to 3 Ripe Haas Avocados

*Note: You will need to make the "Pico De Gallo Salsa" for this dish (see previous page for this recipe). Prepare according to how many people you will be serving.

Preparation:

This is a very simple and healthy dish to prepare. Make your Pico de Gallo first and set it aside.

Slice your Avocado in halves or, in slices (your preference). Scoop some "Pico De Gallo" and place it over the top of your slices of fresh Haas Avocados which you will place on small individual salad plates.

This dish is a very light, refreshing and healthy as a salad or, as a snack to enjoy for yourself or to serve to family and friends. Enjoy!

Presentation of my
Pico De Gallo over Avocado

This is a very refreshing and delicious!

This recipe serves 1 to 2 people.
Adjust according to how many people you are serving.

Mexican Style Shrimp Cocktail

Ingredients: (place each ingredient in separate bowls)

2 to 3 Large Plum Tomatoes finely chopped
2 to 3 Ripe Haas Avocados finely cut into small cubes
1/2 of a White Onion finely chopped
15 to 20 strands of Fresh Green Cilantro finely chopped
2 to 3 Fresh Limes
1 Bag of Frozen (already cooked Shrimp) Small, Medium, or, Jumbo size (your preference)
1 Bottle of "Tapatio" Hot Sauce (measurements will vary depending on each serving
1 Large can of Plain Tomato Juice (for <u>drinking</u> not for cooking).
Please do not use the V-8 Juice for this recipe as it will <u>not</u> work with these flavors.

Preparations:

Chop all the vegetables and place each ingredient in individual bowls for easy access as you prepare to build and layer these ingredients later into each individual serving glass.

Rinse and clean your cooked shrimp. Once clean, place in a medium bowl, squeeze 1 Lime into the Shrimp and let them sit in the Juice until we're ready to start layering the glasses. Place in Fridge to Chill for 15 minutes.

In a large Pitcher, pour half of the can of plain Tomato Juice, add 2 to 4 tablespoons of Tapatio Hot Sauce, squeeze 1 entire Lime into this mixer and mix together. Add salt for good taste.

I prefer serving this special "Shrimp Cocktail" in a tall glass (Ice Cream Float type Glass), see the photo example on the next page. You will layer each ingredient from the base of the glass, all the way to the top of the glass.

Grab your first glass, bowls, Pitcher of Tomato Juice, marinated Shrimp too. Bring everything near you so to start layering the glasses. Start with a small amount of Onions, Tomatoes, Avocado, Cilantro, Shrimp, 3 drops of Lime juice, a splash of Tapatio hot sauce and pour some spicy tomato juice...and repeat this process to the top of the glass. Garnish the top of each glass with Avocado and a squirt of Lime juice, a splash of Tapatio hot sauce! Serve with Ritz Crackers and a long spoon. You will love this recipe!

Presentation of my
Mexican Style Shrimp Cocktail

Serve a wedge of Lime to accompany the crackers served along side this delicious Shrimp Cocktail! Serve with a long spoon. This is one of my all time favorite recipes! I love it!

This recipe serves 4 people (if serving only one serving).
Serves 2 people with second servings. Adjust recipe accordingly.

Soups

Jalapeno & Lime Noodle Soup

Ingredients:

20 strands of finely chopped Fresh Cilantro
2 Limes
1 Garlic Clove finely chopped
1/2 of Cup of finely chopped White Onion
1/2 finely chopped fresh Jalapeno (reserve the other 1/2)
2 Fresh Plum Tomatoes finely chopped
3 Cartons of already prepared Chicken Broth (32 oz cartons)
2 to 3 Tablespoons of Hot Tapatio Sauce
1 Carton of very fine Rice Noodles (I love the Thai Kitchen Fine Rice Noodles for this recipe)
Olive Oil

Preparations:

In a medium soup pot sauté with Olive Oil your chopped Garlic, Onions, Jalapenos, Tomatoes, Cilantro, salt & pepper and allow all the spices to be infused with each other for about 15 to 20 seconds. Now add your Chicken Broth into the pot, add 3 to 4 splashes of Tapatio hot sauce into the broth mixture and allow to cook on medium low heat for about 10 minutes.

Add the extra Thin Rice Noodles into the pot of soup. You can use half of the box of extra thin Noodles (half of a box is quite enough). Once the noodles are cooked, run a knife through the soup to cut the noodles into smaller lengths (this is the easiest way to do this). While the soup is cooking, squeeze the juice from one Lime into the soup mixture too. Stir and cover the pot and allow to cook for about 10 to 15 minutes more on low heat. When you are ready to serve this soup, chop some additional Jalapeno peppers and sprinkle over the top of the soup and also serve with a wedge of Lime and don't forget to offer the Tapatio hot sauce!

Presentation of my
Jalapeno & Lime Noodle Soup

This soup is one of my very own unique creations (one of many), and I truly love it! I love the spiciness to it, and the noodles are so wonderful to enjoy in every spoon full! The beautiful hint of lime within this lovely spicy soup is simply heavenly! I hope you will enjoy this recipe too. ;)

This recipe serves 2 to 4 people.
Adjust according to how many people you are serving.

Spicy Shrimp & Potato Soup

Ingredients:

20 strands of finely chopped Fresh Cilantro
1 Garlic Clove finely chopped
1/2 of Cup of finely chopped White Onion
1/2 finely chopped fresh Jalapeno (reserve the other chopped half for later)
2 Fresh Plum Tomatoes finely chopped
3 Cartons of already prepared Chicken Broth 32 oz
2 to 3 Tablespoons of Hot Tapatio Sauce
1 to 2 Peeled Potatoes chopped in small cubes
2 Limes
1 Large bag of already cooked Shrimp (I buy the frozen and allow to sit in water to defrost)
1 Small Package of Sazon with Saffron (product of Goya)
Olive Oil
Options: This is also delicious by substituting the Shrimp for Chicken (I use a Lemon Pepper Rotisserie Chicken), I take all of the Chicken off the bones for this soup too

Preparation:

In a medium soup pot sauté with Olive Oil your chopped potatoes. When the potatoes are cooked, add the chopped Garlic, Onions, Jalapenos, Tomatoes, Cilantro and sauté for a approximately 15 seconds. Add the cooked Shrimp into the pot and allow to mix and cook while infusing flavors with the fresh herbs for 15 seconds and then add 1/2 packet of the Sazon Goya spice powder (add approximately 1 Teaspoon of the Sazon powder). Continue sautéing for 15 seconds more. Now add 2 to 3 cartons of Chicken Broth into the pot, add 2 to 3 splashes of Tapatio hot sauce and allow the soup to infuse all the flavors together on medium-low heat for 20 minutes. Once the soup is ready, squeeze 1/2 a lime into the soup and taste for enough salt and serve. Enjoy!

Presentation of my
Spicy Shrimp & Potato Soup

You can serve this soup to your guests by sprinkling some fresh chopped Jalapeno over the top of each soup bowl and offer it with a slice of lime to squeeze over top when ready to enjoy.

This recipe serves 2 to 4 people.
Adjust according to how many people you are serving.

Spicy Pinto Bean Soup

Ingredients:

3 Strips of lean Bacon - cut into small cubes
10 strands of Cilantro finely chopped
1 White Onion finely chopped
2 Plum Tomatoes finely chopped
1 Fresh Jalapeno pepper finely chopped (reserve 1/2 for later)
4 Cans of already cooked Pinto Beans (15 oz each can)
2 to 3 Cartons of Chicken Broth (32 Oz)
Tapatio Hot Sauce
Olive Oil
Option: Purchase or make Corn Bread to serve with this soup...very Yummy together!

Preparations:

In a soup pot cook the Bacon to medium crispy and after it is cooked set it aside in a bowl for later use.

Use the grease from the Bacon for extra flavor to sauté the Onions, Jalapeno, Tomatoes, Cilantro for about 15 seconds (or, just use olive oil). Now add the 4 Cans of the already cooked Pinto Beans into the pot to mix with your sautéed vegetable ingredients too. Add the cooked Bacon into the bean soup and 2 to 3 splashes of Tapatio Hot Sauce to blend in. Now add your 2 to 3 cartons of Chicken Broth and allow to cook on medium-low heat for about 20 to 30 minutes. When it is ready, serve this delicious bean soup with some nice corn bread and butter!

Presentation of my
Spicy Pinto Bean Soup

This Pinto Bean Soup can be enjoyed with some warm Corn Bread and Butter as it is simply awesome together! You will love this combo and ask for seconds! Serve this lovely Bean soup by garnishing the top of each bowl with chopped Jalapeno peppers and finely chopped white onions. This will become one of your favorites too. Enjoy!

This recipe serves 2 to 4 people.
Adjust according to how many people you are serving.

Spicy Black Bean Soup

Ingredients:

10 strands of Cilantro finely chopped
1/2 of a White Onion finely chopped (save 1/2 of the chopped onion for later)
2 Plum Tomatoes finely chopped
1 Ripe Hass Avocado sliced for Garnishing the soup (when ready to serve)
1/2 of a Fresh Jalapeno Pepper finely chopped (save the other 1/2 for later)
4 Cans of already cooked Whole Black Beans (15 oz each can)
2 to 3 Cartons of Chicken Broth (32 Oz)
Tapatio Hot Sauce
Olive Oil

> *Option:*
> *Purchase or, make some Corn Bread to serve with this lovely soup.*

Preparations:

In a soup pot, add Olive Oil to sauté the Onions, Jalapeno, Tomatoes, Cilantro for about 15 seconds. Add 4 Cans of your already cooked whole Black Beans. Then add 2 to 3 splashes of Tapatio Sauce to blend and infuse all these flavors together for 15 seconds. Add 2 to 3 cartons of Chicken Broth, salt for taste and allow to cook on medium-low heat for about 20 to 30 minutes.

When this bean soup is ready, serve and garnish each bowl with some chopped Onions, Cilantro, a splash of Tapatio hot sauce, 2 slices of Avocado over the top and also offer a wedge of Lime on the side to later squeeze when your guests are ready to enjoy. Corn Bread with butter goes very with this bean spicy soup too.

Presentation of my Spicy Black Bean Soup

Garnish with two slices of Avocado, chopped Onions, Cilantro, Jalapenos and Crumbled Queso Fresco and a squirt Tapatio hot sauce and serve with a wedge of Lime! Don't forget the Cornbread and butter. Enjoy!

This recipe serves 2 to 4 people.
Adjust according to how many guest you will be serving.

Spicy Corn Soup

Ingredients:

1 White Onion finely chopped
2 Garlic Cloves finely chopped
2 Plum Tomatoes finely chopped
1/2 of a Jalapeno Pepper finely chopped (save the remaining for later)
1 Tablespoon of Cumin Powder
6 Cups of Corn Kernels (can be Fresh or Frozen)
3 Cartons of Chicken Broth (32 Oz)
1/4 Cup of Milk or, Cream
Tapatio Hot Sauce
Salt & Pepper

Preparation:

In a large soup pot, add some olive oil and sauté the Onions, Garlic, Tomatoes, Jalapenos, Cumin for about 15 seconds on medium heat. Now add the Corn and sauté the corn together with the vegetables for 15 more seconds. Bring the heat temperature down to medium-low and pour the chicken broth carefully into the pot and allow to cook together to infuse all of the flavors for about 20 minutes. Add the milk or, cream into the soup mix and allow to simmer for 10 more minutes. Also add any additional salt & pepper and a few splashes of Tapatio hot sauce for extra great flavor. When the soup is ready, serve it hot and enjoy this special recipe with family and friends! For extra spice, you can garnish with extra chopped Jalapenos peppers when you are ready to serve this soup.

Presentation of my
Spicy Corn Soup

When I was around 13 years old, on one of our annual vacation trips to our ranch in Mexico, I remember observing one of our Rancher's wives cooking and making a very spicy corn soup over an open fire. It probably was around the time I must have been intrigued by spices and learning more about my love for cooking. This wonderful woman allowed me to help her prepare and cook this soup and later, she invited me to enjoy a bowl of her very spicy soup. Wow, was it "spicy" but it was also super delicious beyond any words I could try to describe! Throughout the years I have tried remembering what she taught me back then on that early evening cooking with her on an open fire. Enjoy my version of this favorite soup recipe!

This recipe serves 3 to 4 people.
Adjust according to how many people you are serving.

Main Dishes

Spicy Enchiladas

Ingredients:
5 Plum Tomatoes
2 1/2 Cups chopped White Onions
1 to 2 Large Jalapeno Pepper (1 is enough)
2 Garlic Cloves
Approx. 15 strands of Fresh Cilantro (chopped)
1 1/2 Cups Chicken Broth
1/2 Tablespoon Salt (to your tasting)
2 Teaspoons of Cumin Powder
Olive Oil

All of these ingredients go into a blender to blend together to make the spicy Enchilada sauce.

You will also need:
15 to 20 Soft Corn Tortillas (purchase in a bag-local grocery store)
White Mexican Cheese "Queso Fresco" (crumble into a bowl) or,
Four Mexican Cheeses (purchase in a bag-local grocery store)
Crema Mexicana (Mexican Sour Cream)

You will also need:
Tongs or
Large Forks
1 Large Platter
2 large skillets

Preparation:
In a large skillet add your oil, once it is medium hot then add your blended ingredients to cook sauce for about 15 mins. You can tweak the sauce by adding more chicken broth, Cumin, Salt, Jalapenos, Cilantro, etc. to your liking. Once the sauce is cooked, set skillet aside for a moment. Add a new skillet with more oil, on medium heat, toast the soft tortillas gently into "Medium flexibility" but not too soft that they rip on you when you turn them with your fork (or tongs) but not stiff, nor hard. Once both sides of all the tortilla are medium-pliable, stack them all on a plate. Bring your bowl of cheese near the stove to prepare the enchiladas. Bring your sauce back onto the stove to warm up again. Dip each tortilla into the sauce (dip both sides of the tortilla), then lay on platter and add your cheese preference. With a spoon, pour 2 Tablespoons of sauce inside and over the cheese and roll them up and push each one of them to the edge and repeat process. When platter is full, sprinkle extra Cheese over the top of all of the Enchiladas and pour just *a little extra sauce* over the top of them (not too much). Serve the platter after placing the Enchiladas in the oven to melt the cheese for just about 5 minutes. Enjoy!

Presentation of my
Spicy Enchiladas

If you want to explore more cheeses than simply using the Queso Fresco, you can also use the Four Mexican Cheeses sold in a bag from the grocery store and/or make them with Mozzarella cheese to enjoy a different cheese flavor. Explore and enjoy!

This recipe serves 2 to 3 people.
Adjust according to how many people you are serving.

Creamy Red Enchiladas

Ingredients:
8 oz Can Tomato Sauce
8 1/2 oz of Milk
1/2 Cup chopped White Onions (chop 1 Cup for later use)
2 Teaspoon of Chili Powder
2 Tablespoons of Flour (I prefer <u>wheat</u> flour)
3 Garlic Cloves
1 1/2 Cups Chicken Broth
1/2 Tablespoon Salt (to your tasting)
2 Teaspoons of Cumin Powder

All of these ingredients go into a blender together to make the creamy Enchilada sauce.

―――――――――――――――――――――― *You will also need:*

15 to 20 Soft Corn Tortillas (purchase in a bag)
Medium/Sharp Cheddar Cheese (for filling the enchiladas)
1 Cup Chopped Onions (for filling)
Olive Oil,
Onion Powder (for later when making the sauce if needed)

You will also need:
Tongs or Large Forks
1 Large Platter
2 large skillets

Preparation:

In a blender, toss all of the above vegetables, flour and liquid ingredients into the blender to liquefy into a sauce.

In a large skillet add oil, low to medium heat add your blended ingredients to cook into a creamy sauce for 15 minutes while "constantly" using a swifter to keep it from clumping up. If you need to tweak the sauce, add only more chicken broth, Milk, Cumin, Salt, and Onion Powder. Once the creamy sauce is made into a gravy consistency, set skillet aside.

Add a new skillet with new oil, on medium heat to toast the soft tortillas into "Medium flexibility" not too soft that they rip on you when you turn them with your fork or, tongs. Do not make them stiff, nor hard either. Once both sides of all the tortilla are medium-flexible, stack them all on one plate for later assembly use....

Presentation of my
Creamy Red Enchiladas

Continued Preparations…

In separate bowls, have your cheese and onions near the stove to prepare the Enchiladas on a large platter. Bring your creamy sauce back onto the stove to *only warm up*. Dip each tortilla into the sauce (dip both sides of the tortilla in the skillet with the sauce), then lay each individual tortilla on a platter and fill the center of each one with cheese, a little onions and roll them up and push each filled and rolled Enchilada to the edge of the platter and repeat this process. When the platter is full, pour some creamy sauce over the top of the already rolled Enchiladas, sprinkle Cheese & onions over top and place platter in oven to melt the cheese for only 5 minutes (just to melt the top layer of cheese), then serve platter. This was my favorite childhood food. I remember my aunts and cousins cooking this dish with my mother in our kitchen when they all came to visit us in Florida. This recipe will become a favorite of yours too! Enjoy with family and friends.

This recipe serves 2 to 3 people.
Adjust according to how many people you are serving.

Chicken Tacos

Ingredients:

2 Chopped Plum Tomatoes (chop 2 extra Tomatoes for Taco filling)
15 Strands of Chopped fresh Cilantro (chop 10 extra strands for Taco filling)
1/2 Chopped White Onion (save 1/2 chopped Onion for the Taco filling)
1/2 tspn of Fresh Green Jalapeno Pepper (the rest can be sprinkled on Taco)
4 Fresh Limes (squeeze 1 lime into the cooking mix), serve wedges with the Tacos
1/2 of a Sazon Goya w/ Azafran Seasoning Powder packet
1 to 2 Tblspn of Tapatillo Hot Sauce
1/3 Cup of Chicken Broth

Olive Oil
15 to 20 Soft Corn Tortillas (sold in quantities of 20+)
1 Rotisserie Chicken (I like Lemon Pepper), take chicken off the bone and chop too
1 1/2 Cup chopped Cabbage or, Lettuce (both offer distinct and different flavors)
Medium to Sharp Cheddar Cheese or, Queso Fresco (your preference)

> Garnish Tacos with Crumbled "Queso Fresco" & Sliced Avocados!

Preparation:

Sauté in olive oil the following chopped items; Tomatoes, Cilantro, Onions, Jalapeno, Salt & Pepper for 5 mins, then add 1/2 a packet of the Sazon Goya and toss in the chopped chicken and add in the chicken broth slowly so it doesn't get too much liquid. Allow all seasonings to cook together on medium low heat but periodically check to mix the chicken around so its not over cooking. Squeeze some lime juice over the top of the cooling chicken and turn off the heat and allow to sit for 10 minutes. In the mean time, prepare another skillet with oil to create our tortilla shells. Once the oil is medium hot, dip 1 to 2 tortillas at a time to get crispy but not hard. Lay all of the lightly fried tortillas in a stack on a plate. Get a large bowl and toss in all of your extra remaining chopped vegetables for the filling; chopped Onions, Jalapenos, Tomatoes, Cilantro, Lettuce or, Cabbage plus, squeeze one large lime into the bowl mix and toss together with some salt & pepper and set next to your platter where you will now assemble your Chicken Tacos. Place your cooked Chicken in a bowl and the stack of fried tortillas (bring them all near your platter) for assembling the tacos. Take one tortillas and place it on the platter then start by filling it first with your seasoned chicken, then your mixed chopped vegetables, sprinkle white cheese "Queso Fresco" and a sliced Avocado on the top. Once the first one is assembled, push it to the edge of the platter and repeat this process again until the platter is completely full of your delicious Chicken Tacos! Serve a bowl of sliced limes, chopped Jalapenos and Tapatio hot sauce and serve. Enjoy!

Presentation of my
Chicken Tacos

This recipe serves 3 to 4 people.
Adjust according to how many people you are serving.

Tostadas

Ingredients:

3 to 4 Chopped Plum Tomatoes
15 strands of Chopped fresh Cilantro
1/2 Chopped White Onion
1/2 of a Lettuce Head - Chopped
2 Fresh Limes cut in quarters
15 oz Can of cooked Refried Beans (Pinto or Black Beans)

<u>Tostada Vegetable Topping:</u>
Chopped Tomatoes,
Onions, Cilantro,
Jalapeno Peppers
Lettuce or Cabbage
Toss in a bowl, add
Lime Juice,
Salt & Pepper

15 to 20 Soft Corn Tortillas (or, buy the Tostadas already crispy), but re-toast in oven for 5 minutes.
Optional: 1 Rotisserie Chicken (take chicken off the bone and cut into small pieces), or Shrimp too. *(Use recipe from the "Chicken Tacos" to make the chicken and/or shrimp for this additional topping recipe).*
1 to 2 Tablespoon of Tapatio Hot Sauce
Olive or Vegetable Oil

Preparation:
Heat oil in a large skillet to medium-hot (in order to crisp soft tortilla in oil to make hard). *You can also buy the already toasted ones too and heat in oven for 5 mins.* Place all of your crispy tortillas on a platter when complete (to assemble them later with ample space). Now in the same skillet, use only approximately 3 Tablespoons of oil, add your Refried Beans and heat them up on medium high heat so you can spread these beans as a base onto the crispy tortilla to build the Tostadas. These are going to be your basic Bean Tostadas, which are awesome! But if you wish to add Chicken or Shrimp, simply use my Chicken Taco recipe to make the shrimp in the same way for an additional topping for your Tostadas. Once you have your Beans spread on the base of the hard Tortilla, add cheese, (add any extras like Shrimp or, Chicken), add your mixed vegetable toppings (see above), serve with a wedge of Lime and garnish with a sliced Avocado and a splash of Tapatio hot sauce. Tostadas taste <u>best</u> when serving hot (as soon as you make them). Enjoy!

Presentation of my Tostadas

This is a great Vegetarian dish. It is great for making something delicious, simple, special and very quick! These Tostadas, taste best *as soon as they are made*. My Mother would make these on Sundays after church for the entire family to enjoy for lunch and even for dinners. We mostly enjoyed them with refried beans. The vegetable Topping is what I think brings all of these wonderful flavors together especially when you add the "lime juice" mixed in with the "salt and pepper" which enhances the refried beans and the toasted tortilla flavors. Try also sprinkling some fresh chopped Jalapeno peppers over the top. Enjoy!

This recipe serves 3 to 4 people.
Adjust according to how many people you are serving.

 # Fidello
Pronounced "Fi-de-yo"

Ingredients:
Half a (16 oz) Bag of the Fine Egg Noodles
15 strands of fresh chopped Cilantro
2 Chopped Plum Tomatoes
1/2 of one chopped white onion
1 chopped Garlic Clove
6 oz can of Tomato Sauce
1 Tablespoon of Cumin Powder
2 Cups of Chicken Broth
3 Tablespoons of Olive Oil

> Enjoy this meal with some warmed up white flour Tortillas, yum, yum!

Preparation:
In a large skillet add approximately 3 Tablespoons of Olive Oil and bring to medium low heat. Open your bag of noodles and break them down to about 3 inches long and add them into the oil to start lightly toasting the noodles (a light brown). Stir the noodles in the hot oil so to not burn them...we want them only to get toasty. Now move the noodles to the side and make an opening in the middle of the skillet and add your onions, garlic, tomatoes, cilantro, cumin powder, salt and pepper and stir together for less than 5 minutes. Then add your Tomatoes sauce and stir some more and when all of that is all mixed together, add your chicken broth and cover the skillet and allow to cook for 15 minutes and then bring the heat down to medium low to allow to cook the rest of the way. This dish should be a little soupy (but certainly it is not a soup). You should serve it in a medium deep plate which will hold the broth. You should also serve this dish with some warm white flour tortillas (heat them up on a skillet), and enjoy together!

 ## Presentation of my Fidello

To heat up the tortillas, it is best to use a plain skillet to heat them up on your stove. Bring skillet to medium heat and heat each tortilla on both sides and place in a basket or plate with a cloth to hold in the warm moister. This pasta dish was also one of my first favorite pasta dishes as a child. I later learned while doing my genealogy research, that this dish was one of the main dishes both of my Grandmothers would cook for their children too. I love this dish even more now after hearing this story!

This recipe serves 3 to 4 people.
Adjust according to how many people you are serving.

Mole
Pronounced Moh-le

Ingredients:
1/4 Cup of plain Creamy Peanut Butter
1 teaspoon of Cumin Powder
2 to 3 Cups of Chicken Broth (broth from a boiled chicken)
1 slice of toasted bread and cut into small cubes (use all crumbs)
8.25 oz can of "Mole Dona Maria"
1 Onion chopped (for chicken broth)
1 Chicken (to boil with onions and salt)

_____
1/2 cup of Raisins (sauté and blended)
1 Banana (sauté and blended)
2 tablets of Mexican Chocolate (1 inch each for each Tablet) or, any dark chocolate will do too.

> Dissolve chocolate in skillet with chicken broth and then sauté Raisins and Banana, then blend together

Preparation:
In a large soup pot add water and onions, salt, to cook your chicken (which will later be used to go into the Mole). Once the chicken is all cooked save the broth for making the Mole gravy. Take the chicken off the bones for the Mole gravy and set aside or later.

Dissolve chocolate in chicken broth in a separate skillet. Then in a another skillet sauté the Banana, Raisins, and then you can bring them together. Once they are cooled down, blend together in Blender with the extra chicken broth to liquefy. Save for later in order to add into the Mole gravy mixture when we go to make it.

In a large deep skillet, add olive oil to heat up on low, add the "Mole Dona Maria" and add 2 Cups of your Chicken Broth, Cumin powder, your blended Banana, Raisins, Chocolate ingredients, 1/4 Cup of Peanut Butter and add the toasted bread and mix together to create a smooth creamy gravy (medium consistency).
If you need to, add any extra chicken broth to help create this gravy to the right consistency. Once the gravy tastes perfect, add the chicken meat into the Mole gravy (without any bones). Allow to cook on medium-low for approximately 20 minutes. Serve over Mexican Red Rice (the Mexican Red Rice recipe is on the next page).

Presentation of my Mole

This recipe normally has many ingredients and many steps for preparing this dish from scratch but we're using this "Mole Dona Maria" product, because this helps to make this recipe easier even though it is still a little time consuming anyway to prepare but it is worth it if you like Mole. This makes a great meal for a big family gathering! Enjoy!

This recipe serves 5 to 6 people with the Mexican Red Rice.
Adjust according to how many people you are serving.

 # Mexican Red Rice

Ingredients:
2 Plum Tomatoes chopped
1/2 of an Onion chopped
1 Garlic Clove chopped
2 Cups of Chicken Broth
1 Tablespoon of Cumin Powder
Salt (add while cooking for taste)

1 to 2 Cups White Rice
4 Tablespoons of Olive Oil
1/4 Cup of Tomato sauce

> In a Blender:
> Place all of your vegetables ingredients to blend together with some Chicken Broth Cumin and salt.
>
> *Additional Options:*
> *If you wish to eat this rice alone, cook it with some chopped Cilantro and serve it with a wedge of lime.
> *You could also chop some Jalapeno peppers to cook with the rice.

Preparation:
In a skillet add oil and bring heat to medium low, add the white rice (1 Cup for 1 to 2 people), and brown the rice as you keep stirring the rice so not to allow it to burn. Then slowly pour in the blended ingredients into the skillet with the rice (be careful not to burn yourself). If you need to, remove the skillet from the heat while you pour the blended ingredients. Stir and taste (add extra salt or, cumin powder if needed) place a lid to cover the cooking rice and bring the heat lower to cook the rest of the way for about 15 to 20 minutes. At 15 minutes, check make sure your rice does not burn. If it is not completely cooked all the way, just add some more chicken broth or, water and allow to cook for 10 more minutes. This rice can be served with Mole or, served as a side dish with refried beans along side any favorite Mexican meal.

Presentation of my Mexican Red Rice

This recipe serves 2 to 4 people.
Adjust according to how many people you are serving.

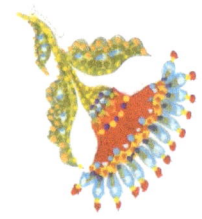

Chicharones Con Chili
(Extremely Spicy)

Ingredients:
2 Jalapeno Peppers
3 Plum Tomatoes
3 Chili de Arbol (Dried Red Peppers)
3 Garlic Cloves
1 Teaspoon Cumin Powder
1 Tablespoon Salt
1 Carton of Chicken Broth (low salt) approximately 32 oz or, you can use water too

---

Small/Medium Bag of "Chicharones" (Pork Rind pieces), sold in a bag at your local grocery stores

Preparation:

In a pot with water, boil your Jalapeno Peppers, Tomatoes, Dry Chili de Arbol, and Garlic (add salt too) boil for approximately 15 minutes until they are soft.

Once boiled, place the boiled vegetables into the blender with room temperature chicken broth or cold water, add cumin powder, salt and blend together. Once blended, taste to see if it needs extra salt or Cumin. Save the blended ingredients in a bowl and set aside for later.

Now in a large deep pot, add olive oil and bring to medium heat. Break all of these "Chicharones" into small bite size pieces and add them into the oil to fry to a medium crisp for about approximately 10 to 15 minutes until they are all toasted.

Once the Chicharones are all toasted, pour your blended chili sauce into the pot with the toasted pork rinds to cook together on medium low heat. Add any extra water or, chicken broth (your preference), into the pot and as they are cooking, add extra water only if it needs extra liquid to make it soupy. Allow to cook on medium-low heat for approximately 15 minutes. These "Chicharones" will become very soft while cooking in this soupy chili sauce. Enjoy with Refried Beans, or, as a side dish. Remember, this is **Super, super spicy but so delicious!**

 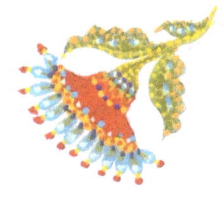

Presentation of my
Chicharones Con Chili
(Extremely spicy)

This is a very authentic side dish that is enjoyed with refried beans and some warmed up corn tortillas or, flour tortillas. If you want to enjoy some refried beans, just buy a can of refried beans and add some olive oil to a skillet and refry them and serve them with this dish to enjoy! This was one of my mother's favorites. She enjoyed with Corn Tortillas and Refried Beans.

This recipe serves 2 to 4 people.
Adjust according to how many people you are serving.

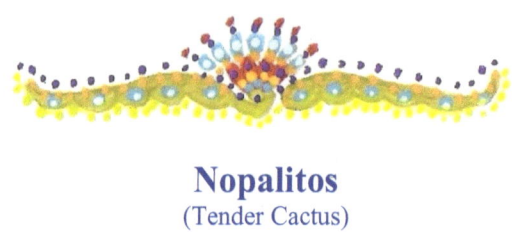

Nopalitos
(Tender Cactus)

Ingredients:
1/2 White Onion Chopped
1 Garlic Clove Chopped
2 Plum Tomatoes Chopped
15 Strands of Cilantro chopped
1/4 Cup of Tomatoe Sauce
1 Tablespoon Cumin Powder

28 oz Can of "Nopalitos" Tender Cactus (drain and discard the juice from can)
1 to 2 Cups of Chicken Broth
Salt and Pepper
Tapatio Sauce
Olive Oil

Preparation:

Open your can of Nopalitos and cut into bite sizes before cooking. You could also cut them while in the skillet too (I sometimes do this). Remember to remove the "Serrano Peppers" as these peppers will make this dish "super hot" and way too spicy to enjoy. You can chop a 1/2 of these Serrano Peppers and it add into the skillet to cook with the Nopalitos. Or, add extra Serranos little by little to your spicy preference.

In a large skillet add olive oil, bring to medium heat and sauté the onions, garlic, cilantro, tomato, add salt, pepper and cumin powder sauté for about 5 minutes. Add the Nopalitos (without the juice from the can), and just make sure they are chopped into bite sizes pieces before pouring your tomato sauce, Chicken Broth, 1 to 3 Tablespoons of Tapatio hot sauce and cook on medium low heat for 15 to 20 minutes. The consistency of this dish is a little soupy. Enjoy with warm flour or, Corn Tortillas!

Presentation of my
Nopalitos
(Tender Cactus)

This dish can also be enjoyed with ground beef. Just sauté your ground beef with chopped onions, garlic, dash of cumin powder, a dash of oregano and salt/pepper and allow to cook for 15 minutes then add into the mix of the rest of the cooking process with the Nopalitos. Garnish with Queso Fresco. Enjoy!

This recipe serves 2 to 4 people.
Adjust according to how many people you are serving.

www.ingramcontent.com/pod-product-compliance
Lightning Source LLC
Chambersburg PA
CBHW060758090426
42736CB00002B/72